The Lord's Goodness

A Book of Remembrance of the Goodness of the Lord

By Emilie A. Parsons

"Many are the afflictions of the righteous: but the LORD delivereth him out of them all."

Psalm 34:19 (KJV)

"...I have chosen thee in the furnace of affliction."

Isaiah 48:10b (KJV)

ACKNOWLEDGMENTS

Thanks to Frank Schulenburg for releasing the photo that appears on the cover of this book of the Saint Teresa of Avila Church in Bodega California under the Creative Commons Attribution-Share Alike license.

Thanks to Sharon Hail (author of "Christ in Me -My Hope") for editing, proofreading and many helpful suggestions.

Thanks to my son Mark Zinzow for text and cover layout, computer support and tutoring.

Ajoyin Publishing, Inc.
P.O. Box 342
Three Rivers, MI 49093
(888) 273-4JOY

TABLE OF CONTENTS

INTRODUCTION

It gives me great joy to proclaim the manifold goodness of the Lord, to give Him glory for the times He has saved my life, for His great faithfulness to bring me through tragedy, for His guidance, for His strength, for His loving kindness, and for His tender mercies. Most of all, I thank Him for this O so great a gift of salvation and for deliverance from twenty years of going the wrong way.

LIFE THREATENING COMPLICATIONS

It was my third pregnancy. My oldest son Mark was seven years old and my daughter, Lisa was three. The first two pregnancies were normal – not so with this one. I was very ill with the life threatening complications of toxemia and preeclampsia. However, I was not aware of the seriousness of my condition during the pregnancy. Every time I had a checkup, I saw concern on the doctor's face. I knew the high blood pressure was a problem. The time came for Steven to be born. The doctor gave me something that made me numb from about the waist down which made it difficult to push when I was instructed to do so. The mirror was set so that my husband could see the birth but I couldn't. I was later told by my husband that the umbilical cord was wrapped around our baby's neck and that the doctor worked very fast to get it off, thus saving our son's life. Later, the doctor expressed that he was very concerned for my life and thought that I would die in delivery. I was not yet born again, but this was the first time that the Lord Jesus saved my life.

When we came home from the hospital, I was up much of the night with our new baby, and then up all day with the older two children. I was becoming more and more exhausted. The combination of giving birth after a very difficult pregnancy and lack of sleep was taking a toll. There was burning pain in my ovaries and uterus. I was so very tired. While making a bed, I would lie down for a second and fall fast asleep. I felt that I was on the verge of a collapse. It was then that panic struck. What if I died? Who would take care of my children when my husband was at work? I wanted to raise them. I remember that moment. I was standing in my kitchen when that thought gripped my mind. Something happened in that moment. I think I had a nervous breakdown that affected my future behavior.

My parents lived in the northern part of the state. Two of my very dear aunts took Mark and Lisa to visit my parents. While they were away, I slept every time the baby slept. Slowly I recovered from the exhaustion, but it was still a struggle. Even though at that time, I was not a born again

Christian, I asked God for help. In His great mercy and loving kindness, He answered me.

Doctors could only offer drugs and surgery, neither of which I needed. Instead He opened up a whole new world to me in the study of nutrition.

After the birth of my first child, Mark, I began having back pain. The doctor I went to gave me a bottle of pain pills and taped up my back. I learned later that my back was out of alignment. Some friends of ours recommended an osteopathic physician who had helped them very much. I did not realize the skeletal structure could be out of alignment, and that it could be treated by certain doctors such as osteopaths and chiropractors. This was back in 1959, and I had never heard of an osteopath. I went to him, and he explained the problem and made the needed adjustments. It was called a subluxation of the pelvis which simply means that the pelvis is out of alignment. Along with that, I had strain in the lumbar and sacral region which is low back pain.

One day after Steve was born, I went in for a back adjustment and discussed my health with the doctor. He advised me not to eat white sugar. He suggested I go to a health food store and get some raw sugar. While at the store, I felt drawn to go

7

over to the bookshelf. I picked up a book entitled <u>Bragg Toxicless Diet Body Purification & Healing System</u> by Paul C Bragg, N.D., Ph.D. I looked it over and purchased it. When I arrived home, I read it and asked my husband to read it too. Wow! I had no idea I was eating disease causing foods. After my husband read the book, we agreed to change our diet and follow the teachings in the book. We eliminated all white flour and white sugar products and processed foods. Discontinuing sugar altogether, raw honey proved to be a good substitute. I was able to purchase it from a bee keeper who lived not far from us. We began eating much more fresh fruits and vegetables. We purchased wonderful raw milk cheese at a health food store, and drove to a farm about thirty miles away to get raw milk from an organic farmer. That was real milk and much healthier than the pasteurized homogenized variety. The farmer's barn was immaculate, and the backsides of the cows were washed before milking. There has to be a very high standard of cleanliness in order to get raw milk. I don't know if it is possible to get milk like that anymore. It tasted like liquid ice cream. The cream on the top was so sweet that it could be whipped and eaten without adding any sweetener.

Our family began to thrive on this new diet of natural foods. My three year old daughter needed to have her tonsils out. They were about the size of golf balls, and three doctors said they had to come out. They said I could not stay overnight with her in the hospital, and I knew she would be very frightened if I didn't. About the time I was faced with this dilemma, we had begun our new way of eating. She ate a lot of fresh fruit and unrefined foods. I was thrilled when I saw that her tonsils were receding, and soon they were back to normal size. She never had to have them out. My husband had acne since high school and that cleared up. My oldest son had a persistent cough caused by post nasal drip which cleared up as well. My husband and I both lost twenty five pounds without even trying to lose weight. We were very pleased with the results of our natural food diet.

My interest in nutrition gave me a desire to know more. It was amazing how I was led to purchase books on nutrition by a wide variety of authors, from medical doctors to nutritionists to journalists investigating the role of nutrition against disease. It was absolutely fascinating to discover the therapeutic value of nutrients and vitamins, and their application to achieve optimum health. Over the years, I acquired quite a large library of books on health and nutrition. It was gratifying to be able to share these exciting discoveries with family and friends. Little did I know how this knowledge would open a new door to work in this field. This was to come about after my salvation.

From the standpoint of nutrition, we were doing very well; however, with the birth of each child my back problems grew worse. I was in pain most of the time. I asked the doctor why I never had any pain in my back until I went through childbirth. He explained that sometimes that happens with tall, slender women. The pelvis separates during delivery, and evidently the ligaments were stretched. At any rate, I was in pain all the time, and there were frequent trips to the osteopath for adjustments. Constant pain takes its toll, and in that respect, life was a struggle.

MY ENTRANCE INTO NEW AGE

Although I went to Sunday School at the Baptist church as a small child, and later to a Presbyterian church, I did not know that I needed to be born again. I learned about God and Jesus, but I did not know about receiving Jesus as Lord and Savior. I did not know the doctrine of salvation, nor did I ever see an altar call. I believed in God but did not know God. As James 2:19 says, "You believe that there is one God. You do well. Even the demons believe and tremble." (NKJV) In John 3:3, Jesus said, "Verily, verily, I say unto thee, Except a man be born again, he cannot see the kingdom of God." (KJV) In verse 5 He says, …"Except a man be born of water and of the Spirit, he cannot enter into the kingdom of God." In verse 6 He adds, "That which is born of the flesh is flesh; and that which is born of the Spirit is spirit." When one repents of their sins and receives Jesus as their Lord and Savior, one is then born of the Spirit. When we are born from our mother's womb, we are born of the flesh, but when we are born again, we are born of the Spirit. Colossians 11:13 tells us that God has then "...delivered us from the power of darkness, and hath translated us into the kingdom of his dear son." (KJV) 2 Corinthians 4 informs us that "...the god of this world hath blinded the minds of them which believe not, lest the light of the glorious gospel of Christ, who is the image of God, should shine unto them." (KJV)

In public high school biology class, I learned about evolution. It was taught as fact, not theory. So I believed in God, but now I had a dilemma. How could evolution also be true? This started my quest for spiritual truth. I began reading a lot of philosophy such as Plato's Republic, Aristotle, Socrates and many others. The answers, of course, were in the Bible, which I would eventually learn. Although I had read in the Bible, I mostly read the gospels and did not have revelation knowledge of Jesus Christ.

My osteopath was president of a New Age group, and through conversations with him, I became interested in his philosophy. I believed in God, but not realizing at that time that evolution was theory and not fact, I thought there was some way to merge my belief in God and evolution. So

I read the books that the doctor loaned me and found the teachings of this philosophy seemed to do just that. One of the books I read was <u>Esoteric Christianity</u>. This intrigued me, and thus began my journey into New Age and away from the God of Abraham, Isaac and Jacob. My husband read the books as well, and we both joined the group. The group we joined encouraged the comparative study of religion, philosophy and science and is a part of what is called New Age. New Age is a broad term that covers a wide variety of sources such as Hinduism, Buddhism, Taoism, astrology, numerology, clairvoyance, yoga, psychics and more. The New Age movement is a broad coalition of networking groups all working for world unity based upon religious experiences and beliefs that have their roots in Eastern mysticism. One of the beliefs I learned about was reincarnation. It seemed to solve the conflict between God and evolution. God set everything in motion and provided the means for evolution to take place. Reincarnation is a doctrine found in eastern religions, such as Hinduism, whereby man evolves to perfection over a period of many lifetimes. Ignorance of the scriptures, of revelation knowledge of God, and not having a personal relationship with Him, leaves one wide open to false religion and false doctrine.

I was not aware of the scripture in Hebrews 9:27 which states that "...it is appointed for men to die once, but after this the judgment," (NKJV) So the God that I first believed in, the God of the Bible, was not the god of New Age philosophy. What I thought was an explanation of my dilemma was really the path down the road of deception and away from truth. I also learned later that although evolution was taught as fact, it was only theory and some of the dating methods used to date fossils were flawed.

In the various aspects of New Age, there is usually some element of truth that attracts a person, but there is much error. Anyone who does not know the Lord Jesus, and is not rooted and grounded in the word of God, would not be able to discern the error. It may sound good, but as the apostle Paul said in 2 Corinthians 11:14: "And no marvel for Satan himself is transformed into an angel of light." (KJV) Once one tenet of their philosophy is accepted, it is like a slippery slope taking one deeper and deeper away from the truth of the one true God, Jehovah.

The New Age worldview is known as Pantheism, the belief that the universe is God, that God is all that exists. This doctrine identifies God with

the various forces and workings of nature. It does
not see God as the personal God of the Bible, the
creator of heaven and earth and all that is in it,
with whom one can have a personal relationship.
New Agers, as a rule, hold the concept of the di-
vinity of the individual, that we are all gods in the
becoming. They seek God within self. However,
the Christian does not look within; he is not centered on the self, but is God centered "Looking
unto Jesus the author and finisher of our faith...".
Hebrews 12:2a (KJV) In Colossians 1:27, the
apostle Paul reveals the mystery heretofore hidden:
"To whom God would make known what is the
riches of the glory of this mystery among the gen-
tiles; which is Christ in you, the hope of glory:"
(KJV) What a glorious revelation! Christ in us!
When we receive Him, He comes to live in us, and
we give Him Lordship of our lives. We are not on
our own, and we do all things for the kingdom of
God through Christ.

In New Age, generally speaking, there is no
personal God, and no personal enemy or adversary. The emphasis is on developing one's own
spiritual nature by right living, meditation, study
and various spiritual disciplines. One must ad-
vance spiritually by means of one's own efforts.
To reach the level of godhood requires many life-

times as one evolves to that level -- thus the teaching of reincarnation. Along with this comes the notion of karma. This is sort of the New Age version of reaping what one sows. One's circumstances in this life are determined by deeds done in a previous life. Good deeds bring good karma, and bad deeds bring bad karma. Eventually, there would be more and more good deeds, and less and less bad deeds, until one finally has no more bad karma and has evolved to perfection, thus attaining godhood. One might say that it is salvation by works. This is diametrically opposed to Christianity. "For by grace are ye saved through faith: and that not of yourselves: it is the gift of God: Not of works, lest any man should boast." Ephesians 2:8-9 (KJV)

Because they must progress by their own efforts, one could say that their righteousness is of the self or self righteousness. This again is diametrically opposed to Christianity. Romans 3:10 tells us … "There is none righteous, no, not one:" and verse 23 says, "For all have sinned, and come short of the glory of God;". (KJV) This is powerfully expressed in Isaiah 64:6a "But we are all as an unclean thing, and all our righteousnesses are as filthy rags;" (KJV) When we receive Jesus as our Lord and Savior, He gives us His righteousness.

God wants all our hope and trust in Christ alone. Salvation is a gift and not a result of our own efforts.

In New Age, God becomes an impersonal force, and evil is a lack of good; thus there is no personal devil. In John 8:44, Jesus spoke these words about the devil: "...He was a murderer from the beginning and does not stand in the truth, because there is no truth in him. When he speaks a lie, he speaks from his own resources, for he is a liar and the father of it." (NKJV) One of his major lies is that he doesn't exist. Lucifer, a created angel, rebelled against God and was cast out of heaven, taking one third of the angels with him. Isaiah gives this account in Isaiah 14:12-15. "How art thou fallen from heaven, O Lucifer, son of the morning! how art thou cut down to the ground, which didst weaken the nations! For thou hast said in thine heart, I will ascend into heaven, I will exalt my throne above the stars of God: I will sit also upon the mount of the congregation, in the sides of the north: I will ascend above the heights of the clouds; I will be like the most High. Yet thou shalt be brought down to hell, to the sides of the pit." (KJV) In Luke 10:18b, Jesus said, "...I beheld Satan as lightning fall from heaven." (KJV)

Scripture refers to Satan as the adversary or the devil as in 1 Peter 5:8: "Be sober, be vigilant; because your adversary the devil, as a roaring lion, walketh about, seeking whom he may devour." (KJV) I did not know that Satan is the "god of this world" and that he has "blinded the minds of them which believe not, lest the light of the glorious gospel of Christ, who is the image of God, should shine unto them." 2 Corinthians 4:4 (KJV)

In the New Age worldview, all religions are different paths to God. This is totally contrary to the words of Jesus in John 14:6: "...I am the way, the truth, and the life: no man cometh unto the father but by me." (KJV) Furthermore, Jesus taught in Matthew 7:13,14, "Enter in by the narrow gate; for wide is the gate and broad is the way that leads to destruction, and there are many who go in by it. Because narrow is the gate which leads to life, and there are few who find it." (NKJV) This statement certainly flies in the face of the present day notion of political correctness which is just another tool of the enemy to deceive. Jesus is the way to Jehovah God, but there are false gods, and the broad way leads to these false gods. This is a powerful scripture in Isaiah 45:5a: "I am the Lord, and there is none else, there is no God beside me:" (KJV)

Finally, and by far the most significant and vital difference between New Age and Christianity lies in the fact that the New Age philosophies are the product of the fallible human mind, while Christianity is about a person: Jesus Christ, the Son of Almighty Jehovah God. The apostle Paul clearly warns in Colossians 2:8 to "Beware lest any man spoil you through philosophy and vain deceit, after the tradition of men, after the rudiments of the world and not after Christ." (KJV) Jesus Christ is deity. The Godhead consists of the Father, the Son and the Holy Spirit. "For there are three that bear witness in heaven: the Father, the Word and the Holy Spirit; and these three are one." 1 John 5:7 (NKJV) Jesus is the Word of God. In Revelation 19:13 we read, "... and His name is called The Word of God." (NKJV) John 1:1 states that: "In the beginning was the Word, and the Word was with God, and the Word was God." (NKJV) Verse 14 declares: "And the Word became flesh and dwelt among us,...". Just think of that! Jesus was God in the flesh: one hundred percent God and one hundred percent man!

One of the names of Jesus is Immanuel. "Behold, the virgin shall be with child, and bear a Son, and they shall call His name Immanuel," which is translated, "God with us." Matthew 1:23 (NKJV)

Matthew was quoting from the prophet Isaiah who, seven hundred years before the birth of Christ, wrote: "Therefore the Lord Himself will give you a sign: Behold, the virgin shall conceive and bear a Son, and shall call His name Immanuel." Isaiah 7:14 (KJV)

He had to be born of a virgin so that he would not carry the sin nature that mankind has had since Adam sinned. In his book, <u>Making Sense Of Spiritual Warfare</u> by Eddie Smith, we read: "When Adam and Eve defied the Lord, sin entered the spiritual DNA of all mankind. From that point, anyone born of a human father would be prone to sin." (page 52, 53)

When the angel Gabriel appeared to the virgin Mary to announce to her that, "...you will conceive in your womb and bring forth a Son, and shall call His name Jesus." Luke 1:31 (NKJV) She asked how that could be since she did not know a man. The angel replied that, "...The Holy Spirit will come upon you, and the power of the Highest will overshadow you; therefore, also, that Holy One who is to be born will be called the Son of God." Luke 1:35 (NKJV)

Although I had wandered in the wilderness of New Age for twenty years, these revelations were soon to come, albeit under very distressing circumstances. When I was involved in New Age, my main interest was in Eastern mysticism. Mysticism is the pursuit of direct union of the soul with the divine that comes through spiritual, not intellectual means. I was looking for this in all the wrong places. I was to find the fulfillment of this through receiving Jesus Christ as my Lord and Savior and learning that I could have a personal relationship with Him. "For in him we live, and move, and have our being;...". Acts 17:28a (KJV)

BORN AGAIN

After all my children were in school, I went
back to school and studied philosophy. After Philosophy 101 and then logic, I took courses in eastern philosophy and studied the primary texts of
Buddhism, Hinduism, and Taoism. In addition, I
studied social and political philosophy. I was deep
into Zen Buddhism when I was shocked to learn
that my husband wanted a divorce. My youngest
son, Steve, had not yet turned twelve years old.
My daughter was going on sixteen, and my oldest
son had just started at the University of Wisconsin.

One day I was talking on the phone to one of
my aunts, a Baptist. As I was explaining my diffi-
culties, she asked me if I would like to receive Jesus. I replied that I would take all the help I could
get. Consequently, she led me through a prayer to
receive Jesus as my Lord and Savior. I said the
prayer with my aunt but didn't really understand
that I had been born again or the significance of
being born again. All this was soon to come
though. Within weeks of that phone call, it be-

came necessary to file for a divorce. I was numb with shock, very frightened and extremely devastated by the emotionally wrenching circumstances. Over a period of time, the shock, the fear and the desolation took a great toll, and I began losing weight. My insides froze, and I could not digest food. I continued to lose weight until I became like a walking skeleton. My parents sent me money to see a lawyer. He advised me to file, before I ended up in the grave. That is how bad I looked. Even though I did not want the divorce, it seemed I had no choice. My husband wanted the divorce. It was unavoidable, and life at home had become extremely unbearable. Not long after that, my husband moved out.

None of the New Age philosophies I had studied had any power to sustain or help me. As a child, I had gone to Sunday school and learned about God and Jesus. Going back to those roots, so to speak, I cried out to God for help. Not long after my pleas, God answered me in an amazing way. I woke up the next morning hearing a scripture playing in my head. It was as if there were a microchip implanted in my brain and I constantly heard: "Seek ye first the kingdom of God and His righteousness and all these things shall be added unto you." Matthew 6:33 (KJV) Keep in mind that I was into Zen Buddhism at the time. I wasn't reading the Bible. After hearing this scripture night and day, I finally cried out to God again and said: "I want to God but I don't know how. Show me how." Shortly after I asked God to show me how; my next door neighbor came over and invited me to a charismatic prayer meeting at his church. Although it was a Catholic church, the meeting was non-denominational. It was not held in the sanctuary. I don't remember exactly, but it may have been held in a classroom. There were sisters there, but the speaker was a lay evangelist. He had owned an electrical business which the Lord had directed him to shut down, so he could go on the road to serve Him. The meeting began with praise and worship songs. Everybody lifted up their hands as they worshiped. I did not have a clue why, but I felt I should do as they did. After the worship, the speaker began to have words for certain people. When he said that there is someone here who needs to let go of the past, I knew it was for me. "How in the world does he know that?" I thought. At this time, I knew nothing about the Holy Spirit and the gifts of the Spirit, but I was soon to learn. At this meeting, I met the most wonderful, Spirit-filled woman of God. She had words from the Lord for me, which absolutely astounded me. I had felt like such a failure because of the divorce, that I could not understand the Lord's acceptance of and love for me. This was all completely new to me.

Also, after the prayer meeting, my neighbor suggested I go to the speaker for prayer as others were doing. After sharing my situation with him, he instructed me to put my hand over my heart, which I did. Then he had his lovely wife put her hand over my hand, after which he put his hand over hers and prayed for healing of a broken heart. It was such a beautiful prayer, and the love I experienced from this anointed couple blessed me so much.

Now I had become thirsty for knowledge of God, and completely captivated by how personal a God He is. When the woman I met who prophesied over me said she was going to St. James prayer group on Thursday, I asked her if I could go with her. She invited me along, even picked me up and took me there. I had no way of knowing what a huge part that prayer group would play in my coming into the kingdom and being delivered from false doctrine, false religion and false belief.

Shortly before going to this meeting, I was shocked one day after taking a shower. I was horrified when I looked in the mirror. I could hardly believe it was me standing there, nothing but skin and bones. Fear struck me. I asked God to keep me alive, at least until my two youngest children were able to be on their own. (My oldest son was in college, struggling to put himself through school. He worked very hard to get through the university, and I am very proud of him as I am of my daughter who suffered many hardships before her graduation from college. She was sixteen at the time of the divorce, and Steve was twelve. Steve was very traumatized by the divorce.)

The meeting my neighbor took me to was on a Monday. I could hardly wait to go to the meeting on Thursday with the woman I had met on Monday. Thursday finally came, and off I went with the woman I met at the prayer meeting on Monday. Again the meeting was at a Catholic church, but held in the school gym. The school was in a separate building behind the church. As I walked into the room, I immediately sensed the presence of God, and I saw a golden glow over the room. I didn't know then, but I know now that it was the glory of God. I had never experienced anything like that before. It was a large room, and there were many people there, probably around two hundred. The meetings were conducted by laymen who were the leaders of the group. There were eight of them if I remember correctly, and they rotated conducting the meetings. These men were what the Bible calls mighty men of God. Their devotion to God, their love, their kindness and humility had a tremendous effect on me. I had never met people like them before. The men who led the meetings were all very successful businessmen who had committed their lives to the Lord, as did their wives. The leader opened the meeting. After greetings and announcements, he turned it over to the music ministry, and we had praise and worship. Well, I just thought I was lifted up to heaven and was hearing angels singing, it was so beautiful. I was experiencing the presence of the Holy Spirit, although I knew nothing about the Holy Spirit then. I did not know that God inhabits the praises of His people, but I sure was experiencing it. I definitely knew something powerful and glorious was happening. I knew nothing about tongues either, but when they began to sing in tongues, I was sure I heard a heavenly chorus. I was absolutely enthralled. Then the Holy Spirit began to move, and people with that gifting gave words from the Lord. I learned these things about the Holy Spirit and the gifts of the Spirit later of course. This was all so new to me, and I knew that I had found what

I was searching for. Actually, I did not find it, but the Lord, the Good Shepherd led me there. I was experiencing the manifest presence of God. Tears silently rolled down my face through the whole meeting. Somehow I did not feel at all embarrassed, nor did I try to stop the flow of tears even though the front of my blouse was soaking wet. Strangely enough, I did not feel self-conscious or that I was in any way annoying anyone.

Various people got up and gave testimonies. At the end of the meeting, it was announced that the prayer room was open so I availed myself of that blessing. The people who prayed for me were very devoted to the Lord and very loving. I felt so accepted. They told me that the weeping indicated that the Lord was doing healing in me. They also told me that I must forgive my husband and that I needed to be forgiven too. As I left the prayer room, the man who was leading the meeting was standing nearby. He came over to greet me and made me feel very welcome. We began to talk and I told him about my situation. I do not know how to put into words the miracle I received when he invited me to return there, and said that they would be my family, and help me in any way that I needed. I thanked him, and as I drove home I thought, "Wow, I have never met people like that before." They knew the Lord and served Him with such reverence and devotion. Driving home, I felt such a sense of relief. That awful fear lifted from me. My appetite returned and I was able to eat and absorb food from that night on. Through them I experienced the agape love of God.

I sure did come back, every Thursday for five years until I moved to Florida. These precious people mentored me and nurtured me.

Shortly after I began attending the St. James prayer group on Thursday nights, the evangelist who spoke at the Monday prayer group was the speaker at the St. James group. What a pleasant surprise to see him and his wife again. At that first meeting I had gone to on Monday night, he gave the word that someone there needed to let go of the past. I was blessed by their ministry that evening. At the end of the meeting, it was announced that he would be at the home of one of the members of the group the next morning and would be able to minister privately to a certain number of people in the time frame he had available. I signed up for that opportunity and arrived the next morning at the member's home. I was shown into a fairly large room where those of us who wished to see him were seated. At the other end of the room, he was seated at a desk at enough distance so that we could not hear the conversation of the person receiving ministry.

When my turn came, I got up and went to sit in the chair in front of the desk. As I sat down, he said that as I came forward, he could see many thread-like lines connecting me to the past. He told me that the Lord offered to sever those connections if I gave my permission. Wow! I thought it was so amazing that the Lord would ask my permission. He is God, He can do anything, but He gave us free will, and He respects our freedom to choose. Of course I said yes, as I knew I needed help to move forward and let go of the past. The evangelist took a napkin and explained that as he prayed for the Lord to sever those lines connecting me to the past, he would tear the napkin in half as a gesture of what the Lord was doing. Isn't that amazing? First I receive the instruction to let go of the past, and then the ability to do it, as the Lord brought forth the ministry through this anointed man of God. Step by step God leads us and directs our paths.

The St. James prayer group presented a seminar, which I took, called "Life in the Spirit", an eight week course teaching about salvation, the

Holy Spirit and the baptism of the Holy Spirit. Meanwhile, the woman who took me to the St. James prayer group told me of another group that met on Friday nights. My hunger to learn and to fellowship, motivated my request to go to that meeting too. That blessed woman picked me up and took me there as well. At this meeting, she introduced me to the spiritual director of the group, a spirit-filled Catholic priest affectionately called Father Dick. He would become very instrumental in my deliverance. Although I was not a Catholic nor ever had been, it just did not matter. These charismatic prayer groups were non-denominational. Even though many of the people were of the Catholic faith, they did not proselytize their denomination. We were all children of God with no divisions, united in the Spirit. Never before had I seen such a reverence for God as I saw in these people. I learned so much just by observing them.

After meeting Father Dick, my friend suggested that I make an appointment to see him. I was coming out of New Age and going through a divorce at the same time. I felt as though my whole life was being unraveled. The person I loved and trusted was no longer there and no longer cared. Then I learned that all my beliefs and spiritual pursuits of twenty years were not of

God. Life as I knew it had come to an abrupt halt. The divorce alone was more than enough of a trauma to deal with. I was shaken to the core. So I made an appointment to see him. I will never forget that meeting. I shared about my circumstances regarding the divorce and having been in New Age. He recommended some books for me to read, and at the end of our meeting, he prayed for me. His gifting was tongues and the interpretation of tongues. After he prayed in his prayer language, the Lord spoke these words to me through the interpretation: "I have rescued you from the prince of darkness; your suffering is little compared to mine. Keep your eyes on Me." The Lord Jesus Christ saved my physical life and my eternal life. I am forever thankful. Glory to God, The Father, The Son and The Holy Spirit!!

As I said earlier, I was taking the Life in the Spirit seminar at the Thursday night prayer group, and the last meeting was the baptism of the Holy Spirit.

The leaders of the prayer group asked that I see the spiritual director before receiving the baptism. Father Dick was the spiritual director of this group as well as the Friday night group. In my whole life, I had not met such a holy man as this devoted priest.

He was the chaplain at St. Camillus Hospital in Milwaukee, and I went to see him there. In our meeting, he asked me what I had believed in when I was in the New Age group and in my studies at the university. I replied, "reincarnation, karma", and as I sat there trying to think of how to categorize the beliefs I had, a very astounding thing happened. Father Dick demanded, "I command you to identify yourselves in the name of the Lord Jesus Christ." Suddenly I named eighteen things. They just came out without any thought or effort on my part. I was thoroughly astounded. Those spirits were subject to the man of God and had to obey just as when Jesus cast out spirits. He wrote them all down. Then he explained to me that every belief is a spirit. He further said that I was not possessed but oppressed by the enemy. He took me through deliverance of all eighteen spirits of false religion, false doctrine and false belief. He commanded each one specifically to leave in the name of Jesus. Now I was ready to receive the baptism. I had already renounced all of the things I had been involved in and repented of them at the last class of the course. I eagerly waited for Thursday night to be prayed for, in order to receive the baptism of the Holy Spirit.

At last, I had found the truth. Jesus is the Truth. As He said in John 14:6, "...I am the way, the truth, and the life. No one comes to the Father except through me." (NKJV)

I had been baptized in water, and now I looked forward to this baptism. As John the Baptist proclaimed in Matthew 3:11, "I indeed baptize you with water unto repentance, but He who is coming after me is mightier than I, whose sandals I am not worthy to carry. He will baptize you with the Holy Spirit and fire." (NKJV)

Thursday night finally came. Those of us in the class were given a separate room in which to pray for the baptism. Instead of the lights being on, candles were lit, and there was a beautiful soft glow in the room. We were very quiet as Father Dick prayed for each individual. Again I will say that I had never met such a holy man as Father Dick. He was humble, but very powerful in the Lord, very anointed. Often I saw him stand and pray for a very long line of people after some of the meetings.

My turn came. I was prayed for, and I received the baptism with three syllables of my prayer language. I thought I was going to have a flowing prayer language like many others, but they told me to keep saying those three and more would be added. I did that and they were right. More was given as I was faithful to say what had been given me when I prayed.

The "Life in the Spirit" seminar was very thorough and gave me a foundation. I knew my mind needed to be renewed to the word of God.

It was a great shock to my system to learn that all I had studied for twenty years was not of Jehovah God. There were two times when I reached a point that I don't know how to explain. I felt as if I were being pulled through knot holes. I needed to speak to someone who had been in New Age and then received Jesus as Lord and Savior. I learned of a man who headed a Christian Apologetics ministry who had been involved in New Age, although in a different area than I was. I think he had studied with a guru. He came to the saving knowledge of Jesus Christ and was a graduate of Moody Bible College. Twice I called him, and he helped me over those humps, so to speak. Talking to someone firmly rooted in Christ, who understood where I had been, helped me through a crisis.

As I stated earlier, my mind had to be renewed to the Word of God after twenty years of study of false teachings. This does not happen overnight.

God graciously gave me five years of concentrated learning. I called it going to the University of the Holy Spirit. It was during this time that I made the commitment to give the Lord the first fruits of my day in prayer and scripture reading, which usually lasted at least two hours. Then I listened to Christian radio. One of my favorites was J. Vernon McGee. In addition, I watched the 700 Club which I joined. I continued to attend the Monday, Thursday and Friday prayer groups and a church not far from where we lived. It was at that church that Lisa, Steve and I were water baptized. I believe it was a Church of God.

WHOM DO YOU TRUST?

In the very earliest days after I received the
Lord and began going to the prayer groups, I had
an interesting experience one day at the grocery
store. This was before taking the Life in the Spirit
seminar and receiving the Holy Spirit. I was reading scripture every day, but it takes a while to read
the whole Bible. I had not yet read Isaiah 47:13
and 14a. "Thou art wearied in the multitude of thy
counsels. Let now the astrologers, the star gazers,
the monthly prognosticators, stand up, and save
thee from these things that shall come upon thee.
Behold they shall be as stubble; the fire shall burn
them;" (KJV) A very close friend of mine was
quite interested in astrology and even did charts,
but my interest was not that great. I just dabbled in
it a little to the extent that every month I purchased
a magazine at the grocery store that contained a
table showing the positions of the planets. So
there I was, a brand new Christian at the grocery
store, putting the magazine in my cart when suddenly the Lord spoke to me. He asked me if I was

going to trust Him or the planets! Immediately I put the magazine back on the shelf and that was the end of that. Never again have I had anything to do with astrology. I put my trust in the Lord.

LISA RECEIVES THE LORD

My daughter had spent the whole summer visiting her grandparents and knew nothing of all these things. When she came home, she asked me what had happened to me. She said that I had changed and remarked that I was not bitter anymore. Well, I was so glad she asked! I took out my Bible, and explained about salvation, that I had received Jesus Christ as my Lord and Savior. I showed her the scriptures, and when I was through, she asked if she could receive Him too, and she did! She was the first person I had ever led to the Lord, and I was so blessed and happy. Shortly after that, my daughter heard about a prayer group for young people of high school and college age in our area. She found out where it was, and asked me if I would take her and some of her friends to attend the group. Of course I said yes, and off I went on Tuesday night with a car full of teenagers. The group was called "The Barn" for a very good reason. It was held in a barn! It was quite a beautiful barn. It must have been remodeled as it was very clean and attractive. It was owned by a wonderful Christian couple who opened it up for the young people. What a joy it was to see all those young people on fire for Jesus. The leader was a college age young man just full of the Lord. I was so blessed by the devotion of those young people for Jesus. I just loved taking my daughter and her friends to "The "Barn" on Tuesday nights, as I enjoyed the meetings very much.

With the addition of "The Barn", I was now attending four prayer groups a week. The Lord opened a whole new world to me. It was a learning and an inspirational experience to fellowship with the different groups of born again, spirit-filled Christians. I do not remember how long I went to all four groups. The St. James group on Thursday night truly became like a family to me. I became very involved with that group, to the eventual exclusion of the other groups. I cannot possibly speak highly enough of these precious people who helped me so much.

STEVE IS BORN AGAIN
AND I CONNECT WITH AGLOW

About this time, a neighbor told us that a Christian musical group called Second Chapter of Acts was performing in downtown Milwaukee. Of course Lisa, Steve and I wanted to go, so off we went with our usual carload of friends. We were all so excited in anticipation as we had never been to anything like it before. The concert was beautiful, and the worship was powerful. At the end of the concert, there was an altar call, and Steve wanted to go up front to receive Jesus. I was filled with joy. We all accompanied him down to the front of the stage where there was quite a crowd, and we surrounded him as he accepted Jesus Christ as his Lord and Savior. How I rejoiced that the three of us were now born again Christians.

We also began to attend a church not far from where we lived. It was a small church, and the people were very friendly. Lisa, Steven and I were water baptized there. It was at that church that I met a lovely sister in the Lord who appeared at my door one day. She said, "Come on, I am taking you to Women's Aglow." (now called Aglow International) I quickly got ready and off we went. Well, I just loved the Aglow meeting. I continued to attend them every month. The speakers were excellent, and the personal ministry was an immense blessing. What a joy it was to discover that Father Dick was the spiritual director of Aglow as well.

MARK'S SALVATION

Mark was actually the first one of my children to be saved. When he was nine years old, he accepted the Lord at a neighborhood Bible study. Since his dad and I were involved with New Age, we really did not understand the significance of Mark's decision. Oh, how I wish we would have.

GOD ANSWERS

During those early months as a new Christian, a neighbor informed me of a course on the Old Testament being offered by a Christian college not too far away. Even with my prayer groups, Aglow, Christian radio, The 700 Club, church and my own daily reading of scriptures, I was eager to learn as much as I could. So I signed up for the course thinking it would supplement the other teachings I was getting. However, as the course progressed, there were things that did not line up with the other teachings I was learning. All the miracles were being explained away as natural oc-currences. For example, it was taught that God didn't really part the Red Sea. At certain times, the water flowed into tributaries that caused the sea level to go down, making it possible to cross over. Some events were being explained away as impos-sible. This brought about a conflict for me as I was learning a literal interpretation of the Bible, except for obvious symbolism as in the book of Revelation.

One day in class the professor was interpreting scripture according to what he called modern Biblical scholars. I knew very well he wasn't referring to any teachers like Kenneth Hagin or Kenneth Copeland or Oral Roberts. So I raised my hand and asked him, "Who are these modern Biblical scholars?" His answer was that that was not an appropriate question for that class. I was totally stunned, and could only wonder why not, as he went on teaching. I had the feeling that I dared not ask though. All I could think about for the rest of the class was that the teachings of those modern Biblical scholars did not line up with what I was learning. When the class was over, I left feeling very upset. After twenty years of false teaching, false doctrine and false belief, I did not want to be deceived again. I was almost in tears as I reached my car. Then I really began to weep and cry out to God. "Father, for twenty years I was deceived by man's teachings, and I want to know the truth. I will only believe it from you, not man. I believe you and trust you, and I'm not leaving this parking lot until I know the truth." As I sat in my car with tears rolling down my cheeks, God answered me. I knew it was God because He spoke to me out of His Word as He had done that first time I had cried out to Him. He said "In the last days men shall have a form of godliness but denying its power. And from such people turn away!" 2 Timothy 3:5 (NKJV) And that is just what I did. I drove out of that parking lot, happy as a lark and never came back.

REPENTANCE AND FORGIVENESS

When I was in New Age, I thought that I was a spiritual person seeking spiritual things. But was I? In the very first year of my Christian walk, I messed up and felt very terrible about it. I knew that I should run to God to confess and repent of my sin according to 1 John 1:9. "If we confess our sins, He is faithful and just to forgive us our sins and to cleanse us from all unrighteousness." (NKJV) As I laid on the floor in my living room for quite some time, weeping in deep sorrow for my sin, something happened that I had never known of before. I literally felt God's forgiveness. It was as if a great burden or weight had been lifted from me. My heart's desire upon salvation was and is to follow Jesus and obey Him. However, that "old man" does not lay down and die the minute we are saved. As Jesus said, "...the spirit indeed is willing but the flesh is weak." Matthew 26:41b (NKJV)

At the moment we are saved, we receive the nature of Christ within us, but we must mature and learn to walk in the spirit. As it is written in Ephesians 4:15, we must "...grow up in all things into Him who is the head—Christ—" (NKJV)

Just think, we have to grow up in the Lord. And isn't forgiveness a most holy benefit? To think that my God would die for me and take upon Himself all my sins! Psalm 103:10-12 is very comforting:

> 10 He hath not dealt with us after our sins; nor rewarded us according to our iniquities.
> 11 For as the heaven is high above the earth, so great is his mercy toward them that fear him.
> 12 As far as the east is from the west, so far hath he removed our transgressions from us.
> (KJV)

Along the way, I acquired a very inspirational book titled God Calling, edited by A.J. Russell. Being able to let go of the past can be a challenge as one presses on. Paul said it beautifully in Philippians 3:13,14. "Brethren, I do not count myself to have apprehended; but one thing I do, forgetting those things which are behind and reaching forward to those things which are ahead, I press toward the goal for the prize of the upward call of God in Christ Jesus." (NKJV) This is one of my favorite scriptures inspiring me to press on.

The book <u>God Calling</u> contains a message for every day of the year from Jesus to two women who prayed together. I found the message of August 20th to be extremely comforting. A portion of that message follows: "...I say to you both, that you are not to dwell for one moment on your sins, and mistakes, and faults, and bad habits of the past.

You must be as one who runs a race, stumbles and falls, rises and presses on to the goal. What avails it if he stops to examine the spot where he fell, to weep over the delay...And I lay it on you as a command-no looking back." Wow, what an awesome word and what great encouragement! I read and reread that message many times, and I go back to it often.

AN INTRODUCTION

It was less than a year after I began attending the St. James prayer group, that I was introduced to a man by the parents of a friend of my daughter's after the prayer meeting was over. He too had been divorced and had recently experienced the ending of a relationship. He was quite depressed, and I felt sorry for him. Perhaps we were drawn together by our mutual experience with divorce and being new Christians. At any rate, we began dating, and about a year later we were married. He owned a plant and tree nursery and also drove an eighteen wheeler truck. He was on the road five days a week, so I was free to attend my prayer groups, Aglow meetings, and to continue my daily commitment to prayer and scripture reading.

I had also started my own business as a distributor of health products. After spending twelve years studying nutrition, this provided a venue to put my knowledge to use.

AN ENCOUNTER WITH GOD

It was in this time frame, about a year and a half after I received the Lord, that a very interesting experience occurred. Scripture tells us to visit those in prison. One day I went to do just that. I arrived early, and while I was waiting for the person I came to visit to be brought down, I opened up the New Testament that I had brought along with me. It opened to the book of Ephesians, so I began reading the first chapter. Shortly after I started reading, something very amazing and unexpected happened. God's mighty presence came upon me in such a way that I hardly know how to describe it. God began speaking to me from the Word as it applied to my life. Tears flowed from my eyes. My whole being was filled with awe and wonder, and I felt like my heart was going to explode. There were questions in my mind that I had only wondered about, but had never taken them to the Lord in prayer. For example, I pondered about why I had to spend twenty years in New Age philosophy before salvation came. Now God Himself revealed to me as I read His Word that I was saved at the appointed time for me. Words cannot express the tremendous joy and ecstasy that overflowed my entire being in rapturous delight. God was speaking to me! Tears continued to flow from my eyes. As I finished the first chapter, I began to notice that the waiting room was filling up with visitors, and I suddenly felt self conscious. I went into the washroom to wash my face and gain some composure. My blouse was quite damp from the many tears, so I tried to dry it with a paper towel as best I could.

When I returned to my seat and resumed reading in the second chapter, the same thing happened as before. The weighty presence of God came upon me, with revelation of the Word and with tears. I decided I was not about to be concerned with what people thought of me; God was speaking to me, and I wanted to hear every word. As I read the second chapter of Ephesians in the presence of Almighty God, as far as I was concerned, there was just God and me in that room. When I finished reading, the presence of God lifted, and just then, the person I came to visit was brought into the visiting area. What an amazing and powerful encounter with the living God of Abraham, Issac and Jacob that was!

Also, in the time frame of the first year or so since I committed my life to the Lord, in my prayers I asked the Lord to open every door in my life He wanted open, and to close every door He wanted closed. A situation that I was uncertain about was a major focus of my prayers. However, His answer did not address that situation at all. Instead the Lord opened a new business door for me, and switched me to a different company. I was very impressed with this company's research and products, and moved ahead with much enthusiasm.

LEARNING THE HARD WAY

My husband, Louie, had decided to grow al-
falfa sprouts in his greenhouse at the nursery, and
insisted that I take over that enterprise while he
was on the road. Although I tried to explain to him
that my back could not handle that physical de-
mand as I had lived over twenty years with chronic
pain, it just didn't seem to register. He had not
lived with me during those years, and had not experienced what I suffered. He informed me that he
was the husband, and I needed to obey him. As a
new Christian, I did what he asked, much to my
detriment. It was not until I had matured more as a
Christian, that I realized that I should not have
obeyed when it was detrimental to my health.
Louie had arranged for someone to help me, but
that person never showed up, so I did the work
alone. This took a terrific toll on my back and
health. Being on my feet four hours at a time further weakened my back, and landed me flat on my
back in bed. When I was able to go back to work,
my husband saw to it that I had help.

THE MOVE TO FLORIDA

Then one day my husband announced that he wanted to move to Florida. Oh, gosh! I hoped it would pass! I surely did not want to leave my home and all my family. I thought he would forget about it, but he did not! I prayed much, hoping he would change his mind. Then one evening at a prayer meeting, I had prayer with the very anointed speaker and received a word from the Lord. He said, "I am leading you and your husband into new pastures." Wow! That sure was an answer, and knowing it was the Lord's will gave me peace about that, but it presented another difficulty. I was very concerned about my son, Steve. The divorce was very hard on him, and rather stunted his emotional growth. Although he had turned eighteen, I knew he was not ready to be on his own, and my husband would not agree to his coming with us. I prayed much. Temporary arrangements were made for Steve, but I felt that I was pulling the rug out from under him by selling the house and moving away. I really felt very torn inside and continued praying about it after we moved to Florida.

Moving away from all of my family to a place where I knew no one was a great shock. My husband moved to Florida first, and started his lawn service business. He found a house for us, and I flew down to Naples to see the house and go forward with the purchase. A storm had just passed through, and he asked me to help him clean up the lawn of one of his customers. We spent part of the day picking up fallen branches and other debris. The repetitive bending and lifting to throw the debris into the container was again taking a toll on my back. Then I flew back to Wisconsin. It was quite late when I arrived home and being very tired, I laid down on the couch and fell asleep. The next morning, I decided to do some packing and went down to the basement. I had planned to get some things of my daughter's together as her dad said he would store them for her in his basement. I proceeded to pick up a box when suddenly terrible pain shot through my entire back. I had never experienced pain like that before. It seemed to be moving up my spine, and I felt as though I was going to pass out. I did not like the idea of passing out on the concrete basement floor. In a brief flash across my mind, I remembered something a lady at St. James prayer group had spoken. She advised that if you don't know what to pray, or if you don't have time to pray, say the name of Jesus. That is exactly what I did, and the next thing I knew I was upstairs lying on the couch. That was the first time that I sprained my back. For three weeks, I had to crawl around the house as it was very painful to walk. Eventually, I was able to go to the chiropractor to get my back adjusted. Moving was a nightmare, as I had about two weeks to pack and be ready. My husband came up from Florida. With the help of my daughter and some relatives, we loaded up his trailer and headed for Florida. As we drove away heading south, I watched my daughter, who had married, heading in a different direction to return home. Watching her drive out of sight pierced my heart with sadness.

Leaving my family and the life I knew was not easy. I also learned that my husband's plan was for me to work in the lawn service business with him. There was no way my back could handle work like that, and I was rather surprised that he would even expect it. He was disappointed that I couldn't, but he was not there when the back sprain had happened. It still didn't seem to register with him the extent of my back condition. One day I was having quite a difficult time, and in my prayers I asked the Lord for help. He gave me a scripture which was such a comfort, that from then on, I was much better able to adjust. My prayers for Steve continued. I was overjoyed when my husband agreed that he could come down and stay with us. Three months after we moved into our new home, Steve drove down with all his earthly possessions in his car. When he showed up at our doorstep, I was thrilled to see him. I thank God that my prayers were answered. We were a family, and my heart rejoiced to have Steve with us.

When Louie had come down ahead of me to start his business and find a house for us, he had also found a wonderful church. I loved the church and the pastors. I was so blessed as people reached out to us, and we began to meet people. Eventually, Louie and I became involved with the prayer room ministry.

I met a lovely sister in the Lord who invited me to the Aglow meeting, and I was very glad to connect with Aglow again. And so we settled into our new life in Florida.

MY DAD'S PASSING TO ETERNAL LIFE

I continued my commitment to give the first fruits of my day to the Lord spending the first two hours in the morning in prayer and worship. My heart overflowed with thanksgiving for all the Lord had brought me through: Steve's birth, the divorce, deliverance from New Age and the great miracle of salvation. I was not aware that in the not too distant future, He would be bringing me through another very difficult valley.

This occurred in July of 1989. Louie's grandson came down from Wisconsin for a visit, and we took him boating down in the Keys. We had been gone for several days during which time my mother was trying to call me. We did not have cell phones then so she could not reach me. When we returned home, I learned that my dad had passed away. I was very close to my parents. No one could have had more loving, wonderful parents than I had. The funeral service was the next day. I had to make arrangements to fly to Wisconsin right away. Louie's grandson would only have stayed two more days so I spoke to Louie about letting his daughter know that he would be home two days early. I was stunned when Louie informed me that he was not going with me to my dad's funeral. He said he wanted to take his grandson out boating instead. We had just spent several days boating, and I really needed him to be with me at this time. His grandson could come back anytime, but this was a one time occurrence. My plea fell on deaf ears, so I went up to Milwaukee by myself. I had to go through the Atlanta airport. Never having been there before, I was very confused. Struggling to hold back the tears, I asked for help to get to the tram and find my way to my connecting flight. I wished Louie had come with me. At that time, I did not have a suitcase on wheels, so it was quite difficult carrying my suitcase and finding my way. My uncle and mom met me at the airport, and I was so happy to see my mom and tell her I loved her. The funeral service was very nice, and many relatives and friends were there. I was glad to have some time to spend with my mom before I returned home. My hope was to bring her to Florida for the coming winter. As I returned home, I thought about having Mom with us for the winter, but that was never to be.

When my dad retired, he and Mom bought a resort in northern Wisconsin. It had three cottages which they rented out during the summer. Eventually, one of my uncles purchased the largest cottage. Both of my brothers bought land next to my parents land and built houses. My oldest brother, Glen, moved up there after he and his wife, Pat, retired. My younger brother and his family came up on weekends and holidays. My parents were very happy having their two sons right next door. We had many wonderful family get-togethers there in the summertime.

MOTHER'S PASSING

Mom and I always had a phone visit on Saturdays, which continued until just a little over two weeks after Dad died. At this time, my older brother, Glen, called to let me know that Mom had become ill and was taken to the hospital. He did not yet know what was wrong, but would let me know when he had news. One evening when I could not reach my brother, I called the hospital and inquired about my mother's condition. I was told they were doing everything they could for her. That just didn't sound good to me. I continued my prayers for Mother's healing. I was right in the middle of praying for Mom when the Lord spoke to me and said, "Ask Me to give her the desires of her heart." When He instructed me to ask that, I knew immediately that the Lord would take her home because she would want to be with Dad. I obeyed the Lord and prayed as He asked me to. It was just three weeks to the day of my dad's passing that Mother died, or should I say, was graduated to heaven.

This time Louie was able to go with me to Mom's funeral. I appreciated that I did not have to take that flight alone again. As with Dad's service, many relatives and friends gathered to say good-bye to Mom. During that time. I talked with my younger brother, Dennis, and his wife, Eileen, who were with her in the hospital when the Lord took her. She was on a ventilator when it happened. They told her she was a wonderful mother and grandmother, and if she wanted to go, it was al-right. Even though she was on the ventilator, she went home to her reward and to be with Dad. Death only separated them for three weeks. As I said before, no one could have had a better mom and dad than I had. I missed them terribly. There seemed to me to be a very huge empty space in the world.

Our flight back home to Naples was at night, so it was late when we arrived home. The next morning upon arising I entered into my time with the Lord. I began to give Him my deepest gratitude. Because of His willingness to suffer and die as He did, I knew I would see my parents again in His kingdom. As I was thanking Him and worshiping Him, He quickened a scripture to me. "...I am the resurrection and the life. He who believes in Me, though he may die, he shall live. And whoever lives and believes in Me shall never die. Do you believe this?" John 11:25,26 (NKJV) Oh yes, my Lord and Savior, I do!

A BAD MISTAKE

One evening, about a year later, I was cleaning up after dinner. I dropped something on the floor, and I turned as I bent down to pick it up. I felt my pelvis rotate and knew I would have to get an adjustment the next day. However, I did not bargain for what happened later that night. I was in the shower, and as I lifted my foot to wash it, my back sprained really badly. I panicked as fear of having the pain I experienced a few years earlier in Wisconsin came over me. I had an inversion swing that one hangs upside down on to realign the spine. When I had the sprain in Wisconsin, the chiropractor told me that I could not "hang" with my back in a sprain. However, in my panic I erroneously thought that if I would "hang", my back would realign, and the pain would go away. What a mistake! The next morning I could not walk or even get out of bed. It was scary! My husband was really worried, and I guess he finally realized I had a back problem. He called my friend Kris for advice. She suggested he take me to a chiropractor she knew. He had to get me out of bed, dress me and carry me out to the car. The chiropractor put some pads on my lower back that had some kind of mild electrical charge. That was on Monday, and he took me every day that week. It really worked because in one week I was able to walk fairly well.

One day as I was resting in bed, the phone rang. It was to my right on the other side of the bed. I was lying on my back. So to answer the phone, I reached over my body with my left arm thereby twisting my upper body. Big mistake! As I did this, I felt a strange sensation go all the way up my spine, which made a noise that reminded me of a row of dominos falling in rapid succession. Up until that time, all the pain was in my lower back. Whatever happened when I reached over with my left arm twisting my back caused a whole new set of problems. After that, I had tormenting muscle spasms from the top of my neck to the bottom of my spine. I was not able to get an adjustment for some time because of the sprain and severe muscle contractions caused by "hanging". When I finally was able to get an adjustment, the doctor advised me to take two ibuprofen in the morning, two at noon and two at night for the pain. Prior to this time, I had not taken pain medication. At this point, it was necessary. However, I did not realize the danger of taking it on a long term basis. I continued on this regimen for about nine years, not realizing the harm it was doing.

DEATHLY ILL

One morning in the year 2001, I woke up with a terrible headache. I ate an apple to have something in my stomach and took some ibuprofen. Then I became very nauseated and experienced a very violent upheaval as my stomach contents were emptied. I had no idea of the ordeal ahead of me.

Not long after this incident, the Lord impressed upon me to stop taking ibuprofen. I stopped taking it, but wondered what I would do for pain. The next thing I experienced was some inappropriate bleeding. At this time, I did not have a doctor as my osteopathic doctor had moved away due to a family emergency. An osteopath is trained in medicine as well as in spinal manipulation. He had left the name of another osteopath, and I made an appointment with the nurse practitioner. She prescribed a steroid drug which worked for awhile, but then the bleeding returned. I was referred to a gastroenterologist for a colonoscopy. In the meantime, I was having some discomfort in my bladder, so an antibiotic was prescribed. The colonoscopy revealed some ulceration, and another steroid was prescribed. It caused serious side effects and had to be stopped after three days. It seemed to also bother my bladder, and another antibiotic was prescribed for a bladder infection. Now I have had two antibiotics and two steroids. I will comment on the significance of this presently.

All during this time, I was losing weight. I was not trying to, as I was at my proper weight when this all started.

Because of the bladder irritation, the gynecologist ordered a cystoscopy of the bladder. Since the colonoscopy had revealed some ulceration, the gynecologist wanted to make sure there was no ulceration in the bladder. The cystoscopy did not reveal any ulceration; however, after this procedure was done, I had terrible pain in the urethra and bladder. So back to the urologist who prescribed another antibiotic. This caused terrible burning in the urethra and bladder.

One day I was discussing this problem with the clerk at the vitamin store. We agreed that the antibiotics had caused a yeast infection, and the cystoscopy of my bladder got it into the bladder and urethra. This caused the burning and stinging in the urethra and pain in the bladder. She said I needed to go on a special diet and loaned me her book that described the diet.

On my next visit to the urologist, I explained to him that I couldn't continue taking the antibiotic because of the yeast. It made the pain worse. Before I could say anything more, he started yelling at me as he asked me, "Do you always diagnose yourself? Do you always not do what your doctors tell you? If you don't do what I tell you, I can't treat you!" He was positively nasty. I was so very weak and in agonizing pain. I had lost so much weight that I looked like a walking skeleton. I could hardly believe the nasty and outrageous outburst of the doctor. I absolutely could not take the antibiotic. I tried and it made it worse. Needless to say, I did not return to him.

Still I kept losing weight and did not know why. The gastroenterologist ordered an ultra sound which did not show anything wrong, and yet something was terribly wrong. How long could I go on this way?

Thus started my quest to find someone who could help me. I went to numerous doctors and health practitioners. One gynecologist gave me some ointment that relieved the burning in the urethra. Another doctor spent several hours telling me to "feel the pain". He was useless. He just talked but did nothing. I also went to a Naturopath and a grumpy and gruff chiropractor. Eventually I did find a good chiropractor. A few years before all this I went to a rolfer because of the chronic back pain. Rolfing is a technique that releases chronic restrictions, realigns posture and relieves pain. I went to see her, and she recommended that I see a therapist who did visceral therapy. I did not know such a treatment existed. I did see her and was quite amazed at what she could do. She said parts of my intestines were frozen and parts in spasm, and in general, they were all mixed up. There are sphincters in the intestines that need to be all going in the same direction, and mine were not. She corrected that and fixed the other problems. She helped me a great deal. After she did everything she could for me, she sent me to another physical therapist with much more advanced training than she had.

This therapist is a spinal specialist in addition to many other skills that I never even knew existed. I still go to this therapist to this day.

Then one day my husband was shopping and ran into Mr. Robert Johnson, founder of Sky Angel, where I had worked part time for awhile. My husband related the situation, and Mr. Johnson gave him the names of his doctors. Finally, I had good doctors!

I went to the internist, and she diagnosed me with malabsorption. However, the problem with the pain in the urethra complicated the situation. If I took anything different from my regular diet, it would cause that pain. So there was really nothing she could do.

The new gastroenterologist did an endoscopy which revealed gastritis, but we still did not know why I kept losing weight. By October I was still in a lot of pain in the bladder, and began to feel that I was near the end. In a phone conversation with my son, I expressed the fact that I felt it was my time. My husband and I were both exhausted, and there just didn't seem to be an answer.

My dear son came down from Illinois and took care of us for a week. He did everything. And what a great cook he is! He just took over and we ate very well (although I still did not gain any weight). He did everything. What a blessing!

I was supposed to have another test, but the bladder pain and being so thin and fragile prevented me from going.

My daughter and her husband came down from Wisconsin, and again, they just took over. It was Christmas! They bought a tree and the trimmings, and made Christmas for us. We would not have had a Christmas without them. My daughter also went to see a homeopathic doctor about my condition. Lisa arranged for me to go. The doctor helped me very much. She gave me a remedy that healed my bladder in time, and what a relief that was. I went to her until she moved away. By that time, there was no more pain in my bladder. I am so grateful to my son and daughter and son-in-law. They did everything they could to help, and I thank God so much for them. I could not ask for more wonderful children.

I became so fragile that I could not do a chiropractic treatment. We still did not have an answer to the weight loss problem. But God is so faithful. About this time, a very dear friend and sister in the Lord arranged a meeting for me with a retired doctor and his wife whom she met while at the YMCA. She talked with them, telling them about me, and they agreed to see me at their home. This was a divine appointment and what a wonderful Christian couple! God provides! He was a retired Naprapath. I had never in my life even heard of naprapathy. It is a completely different way of adjusting the spine than osteopathic or chiropractic manipulation. "Naprapathy is a branch of alternative medicine therapy that focuses on the evaluation and treatment of neuro-musculoskeletal conditions. It was founded in the early 1900s by Dr Oakley Smith, an early chiropractor. Naprapathy is a derivative of osteopathy and chiropractic which focuses on the spine and subluxations". (misalignments). (*Wikipedia*)

I had become too fragile for regular chiropractic treatments, but this naprapathy was so incredibly gentle. God is so awesome. He sent me a wonderful, compassionate Christian doctor. Because of the weight loss I had very little, if any, muscle holding me together. This was the perfect treatment for me. Even though he was retired, he agreed to treat me out of the goodness of his heart. He and his wife were a huge part of this time in my life. This is a Jeremiah 33:3 answer to prayer. "Call unto me, and I will answer thee, and show thee great and mighty things, which thou knowest not." (KJV)

Earlier I related that in October of 2001, I informed my son that I thought it was my time. In February of 2002, a dear sister in the Lord from my church called me and said that the Lord told her to tell me that it wasn't my time yet. Wow! Not my time yet! I felt that I was on quite a wild ride, but I was holding on to Jesus all the way. My motto was: "For to me to live is Christ and to die is gain." Philippians 1:21 (KJV)

Previously, I conveyed that I had two antibiotics and two steroids and would comment on that presently. Actually, it was more like three antibiotics. Anyway I learned from my physical therapist, who is also a doctor of Chinese medicine, that the yeast caused by the antibiotics had mutated into a voracious strain of fungus caused by the steroids. The antibiotics kill all the bacteria. Without the good bacteria, yeast develops. The steroids proliferate it. It was systemic. I also mentioned that I had learned of the proper diet for this condition, which I was following. Since sugar feeds the yeast, all sugar had to be eliminated, including fruit. It also had to be low in carbohydrates. My diet consisted of plain yogurt containing live cultures of probiotic for breakfast. For lunch I had chicken, fish, turkey or beef and a vegetable and the same for dinner. I was on this diet for several years. I still have to be careful about sugar because that strain of fungus became dormant, and sugar would cause it to return. I don't ever want to have that tormenting stinging and burning again.

I was on my way in dealing with the yeast/fungus infection, but still had no solution to the malabsorption. I prayed all the time and asked the Lord, "If it is not my time yet then how do I get well?" One day I was in the shower reciting the 23rd Psalm. When I got to the part about "yea, though I walk through the valley of the shadow of death, I will fear no evil: for though art with me; thy rod and thy staff they comfort me", the Lord gave me laughter. There I was in the shower, shouting with laughter. (See my book on Travail[1]) I felt such a joy of the Lord, and of course the joy of the Lord is our strength. This encouraged me, and I knew to wait upon the Lord. I love the promise in Isaiah 40:31. "But they that wait upon the Lord shall renew their strength; they shall mount up with wings as eagles; they shall run, and not be weary; and they shall walk and not faint." (KJV)

Meanwhile, I came across some information on the ibuprofen that I had taken for quite some time. I learned that it can cause stomach ulceration and is corrosive to the digestive tract. I believed the malabsorption was caused by using the ibuprofen for too long.

---

[1] TRAVAIL: Powerful Supernatural Prayer, Emilie A. Parsons, Ajoyin Publishing, Inc.

The Lord had said it wasn't my time yet, so I knew there was an answer. I just didn't know what it was.

Then, almost ten months after He told me it wasn't my time yet, the answer came. One day when I went to the naprapath for an adjustment, he told me he had done some research and advised me to take a certain all natural supplement. He said it was healing to the intestinal tract. So I did take it.

WOW! Jeremiah 33:3 again. As soon as I began taking it, I started gaining weight. Hooray! Thank you Jesus and thank you doctor. It took about four months to regain my weight and my strength.

It was wonderful to be able to go to church again. After the service, there are precious saints who serve in altar ministry, so I went up for prayer. I had prayer with a very gifted woman of God, and she had words from the Lord for me. He said, "I preserved you. I held you in My arms. When you were weak, I gave you strength, and when your work is finished, I will take you unto Myself." Even right now I cry tears of joy and thanksgiving. How great is our God! There is none like Him!!!

Glory to God! This is the third time the Lord saved my life.

MARCH 1996

My son Mark was spending a week of vacation with us. By this time, Steve had purchased his own home and lived only a mile away from us. I loved having him nearby. It seemed that whenever I baked bread or cookies he could smell it at his house and always showed up ready to partake with us.

On this particular morning of March 23, Mark and I were just leaving the house to do an errand. Louie was out front working on his lawn equipment.

A man and woman drove down our driveway and got out of their car to talk with Louie. I did not know who they were, and thought they were people my husband knew. As Mark and I were about to get in my car, Louie called to us not to leave. I said we would be right back, but he was emphatic that we not leave. At first I thought he wanted to introduce us to his friends, so we all went into the house. The man introduced himself

78

and said he was a police officer off duty. The woman knew Steve, but I had never met her before. As soon as the man said he was a police officer, I asked him if it was about my son, Steve, and he said yes. Somehow I already knew, but I blurted out the question: "Is Steve dead?" He said yes, and I fell to the floor weeping. From that point everything was a blur. I was too stunned, too filled with grief to function. As I laid on the floor weeping unconsolably, Mark tried to comfort me. He sat on the couch near me and gently rubbed my shoulders. Little did I know that God had brought him to us at a time of such great need. Louie, the police officer and the woman were talking, but my mind shut everything out.

Later some very dear friends came over, and although I got up to speak with them, the shock overwhelmed me. I went back to my place on the floor and wept. Our dear friends discussed something with Louie, but I couldn't participate. My mind was numb. My heart was broken. He was my "baby" so to speak. His twenty ninth birthday was coming in two months. How could he be gone?

My faith in God was very strong. The many times I was in His presence during intercession brought a closeness, a love, and a great reverence for God. (See my book on Travail[1]) I did not ask why. God is good and He is sovereign. His ways are above ours. (Isaiah 55:8,9) My love for God was in no way affected, but my emotional pain was unbearable. Through my sobs I whispered, "I don't want to be separated from him Lord, could I come too?"

Later in the day, I managed to call a close family friend and sister in the Lord, Kris Guy. Her answering machine picked up the call. The following is what she experienced when her phone rang. (These are her own words.)

"The scream of the voice on the answering machine told me there was a death in the family. I couldn't pick up the phone, because I was hysterical. I ran to the farthest room in my house and cried out to God, 'why didn't You tell me, why didn't You tell me? You have to prepare me. Tell me who it is'. After weeping and talking to Him for awhile, the Holy Spirit gave me a calm, and I was able to go to the phone and call Emilie. When she answered, she said 'It's Steve, it's Steve, it's Steve.' After we talked, I went back to that room and started praying for Emilie to live. I saw her ly-

1   TRAVAIL: Powerful Supernatural Prayer, Emilie A. Parsons, Ajoyin Publishing, Inc.

ing on a cold stone slab cut in half from her head down to her belly, and I knew she was on the precipice of life and death. I zeroed in on the very last cell that was holding her together and prayed that the Lord would strengthen that cell and hold it together so that she could mend. I covered that cell in prayer; I soaked it and stayed on it a long time. I was adamant. I prayed that God would give her strength to lie perfectly still. She later told me that she laid on the living room floor all day weeping and telling God that she did not want to be separated from Steve and could she come too."

Kris and her daughter, Gabrielle, drove down from Fort Myers. We all sat together, just stunned. After Kris and Gabrielle left, I called Father Dick and told him what had happened. He prayed for me and received tongues. The interpretation was, "Your son is with Me. Don't ask why, don't ask how, I do all things well."

Then I felt a surge of God's presence and power. It was as if He swept me up into His arms and filled me with strength and joy. Then the Holy Spirit gave me a song. I jumped up from the floor where I was sitting, raised my hands and sang; "He's alive, He's alive, my sins are all forgiven;

heaven's gates are open wide; the Lamb of God has risen; He's alive! He's alive! Jesus is alive!" I kept singing it over and over; and as I sang, there was such a powerful presence of God filling me, lifting me, delivering me, strengthening me and giving me peace.

It was late, about 10 PM. I had not eaten all day. After the Spirit lifted, I suddenly felt hungry and ate some dinner. I know I received a great deliverance and the strength to go on.

The next morning sister Sheila (now Reverend Sheila) called and gave us a scripture which was very comforting to us. "The righteous perisheth, and no man layeth it to heart: and merciful men are taken away, none considering that the righteous is taken away from the evil to come." Isaiah 57:1 (KJV) Also that morning my dear friend and sister in the Lord, Lois Grider arrived at our house with her son, Jeff, to bring comfort and consolation. Lois took me under her wing for quite some time to help me. She was teaching a course at our church called "Women of Promise", and I went every week.

I am so thankful for all those who participated in the memorial service at church. I was still quite numb, not thinking of everything that I needed to do. The days ahead were not easy.

As I removed Steve's belongings from his house, memories flooded my mind, and I missed him so much. Then the Lord gave me another word that kept me going. He indicated that there were still things for me to do and then said, "A mother's love is great, but My love exceeds your love as heaven exceeds the earth. The time of the separation is as the blink of an eye in terms of eternity."

The day I heard the news of Steve's death, I was so shocked and devastated that in my grief, I spoke to my heavenly Father that I could not bear to be separated from him and could I come too. What a beautiful response to my prayer. What happiness to know that Steve was receiving that great love that exceeds mine as heaven exceeds the earth. And then God answered my cry about not wanting to be separated from Steve by telling me that the "time of the separation is as the blink of an eye in terms of eternity". "The blink of an eye". I thought to myself, "I can do the blink of an eye". Yes, it's just "the blink of an eye". I can do that! Oh, isn't God just too wonderful for words.

It was around this time that I remembered a recent prayer time with Kris. Kris and I prayed often for Steve. He had endured many difficult challenges and disappointments. On this day when we were praying, Kris had a vision of Steve being lifted up and out by two angels, one under each arm. His feet were not touching the ground, which was totally burned, as though destroyed by fire. There were burned trunks of trees and burned trees all around. The mountains in the distance had burned trees. Tree stubs behind him were charred and burned. Kris said it was like a picture in a book, like a page in the book of his life. She asked God to show her what was on the next page. Then she saw Steve in a motor boat going down a river. He would stop at a dock picking up supplies, then continue on his way. The scenery was very beautiful, green trees, lush foliage. He was content.

When Kris first had this vision, we felt that something good was ahead for Steve. Little did we know that the Lord was showing us his death and the beauty and joy of being in God's kingdom.

Once again the Lord God Almighty gave me the grace, the strength and the power to live. I am awed by God's great compassion, understanding and tender mercies. My heart overflows with gratitude and love for Him.

On the one hand, I rejoiced that my son is with the Lord, but on the other hand, the pain of missing him was my daily companion. My heart ached as memories of him flooded my thoughts every day.

One day, not long after Steve's death, I was walking my dog when I suddenly began singing a song. Then I realized that I had never heard that refrain before so I asked the Lord if He just gave it to me. I received laughter which meant yes. In the months to come, He gave me more verses, one at a time, until I had nine verses. I will just share the words to the first verse here. "I love You Lord, I love You Lord, much more than I can say, I love You Lord, my love for You grows stronger every day."

Speaking of walking my dog, there is a story about him. He was Steve's dog. Steve got him from the Humane Society when he was a puppy, and named him Ruger. Mostly, we called him Rugie. Since Steve was gone all day working, he asked me to puppy sit. I kept Rugie with me when Steve was gone. I soon became quite attached to him, and eventually asked Steve if I could keep Rugie at our house. I will never forget his reply.

He smiled the sweetest, cutest and just slightly mischievous smile and said, "I thought a dog would be good for you, Mom." He knew if he had just come home with a puppy and handed it to me, I would have fussed about how could I take care of a dog considering my back problems and so on. So instead, he got the puppy and let me fall in love with him. I always loved dogs and had one most of my childhood. I discovered that I could manage taking care of a dog. In fact, walking him actually was good for my back. I was quite impressed with Steve's good psychology.

Rugie adored Steve, and whenever Steve came over, Ruger was right up on the couch sitting next to him. After Steve's going home to be with Jesus, Ruger did not understand why he didn't see him any more. Every time I walked Rugie down the street, he would stop if he saw a white pick up truck like Steve had and watch to see if it went in our driveway. He did that for years.

Louie and Steve had become quite close, and it hit him hard too. Louie's sympathy was very touching. In memory of Steve, Louie decided to give Ruger a rub down every day after he came in for the day and took his shower. Ruger loved having his back scratched. If I were sitting in my chair, he would back up to me so I could scratch his back. He just loved it when Louie gave him his rub down. He would wait outside the bathroom door while Louie took his shower, then follow him into the bedroom to get him to hurry and dress. When Louie was dressed, he would run into the family room and get into position for his rub down, which he relished. It blessed me to watch the whole thing, which was a daily and most happy ritual in our house.

About a year after Steve was taken home to be with Jesus, I was in church, and we were singing a song based on Psalm 30, verse 11. "You have turned for me my mourning into dancing; You have put off my sackcloth and clothed me with gladness." (NKJV) As I was singing, I felt all the grief and sadness in my heart lifted out of me after which my whole being was infused with joy unspeakable. Joy! Joy! Joy! Glory to God!

FACING ANOTHER DEATH

Previously, I discussed my bout with malabsorption which began in May of 2001. By April of 2003, I was recovered. During the time that I was ill, my husband became ill as well. It was quite difficult that we were both struggling at the same time. Louie underwent surgery which had a very bad outcome. By the end of 2003, he was not able to work anymore. Over the next two years, he was in and out of Cleveland Clinic with serious health issues as a result of the surgery. In February of 2006, he succumbed to the illness and died. Even though I had been prepared regarding the time he had left, it was still hard to deal with.

Immediately following my husband's death, there were other matters to cope with as well. One of them was the necessity to get the house ready to sell. The Lord instructed me to call Lois, my friend and sister in the Lord, who is also a real estate agent. Once again Lois was an enormous help, not only regarding the selling of the house, but also on another matter. The Lord intervened on my behalf in an amazing way which allowed us to concentrate on the sale of the house.

Lisa and her husband came down from Wisconsin to help clean out the garage and Louie's shop. There was so much stuff to get rid of. They had a dumpster delivered and hired people to clean out the shop and garage.

When we built our new garage, we built a small apartment on the back of it, with the idea that my parents might one day come and stay with us. However, that was not to be. One of the rooms was filled with things of Steve's. They emptied all of that out of the room. When I walked in and saw that everything was gone, I thought my heart would stop; it was such a shock. In some way or other, having those things of Steve's there was a comfort, a reminder of him. Steve had worked as a carpenter and built some of his own furniture. A table and four chairs and a corner bookshelf that he built were in that room. Also his dishes, pots and pans, a bowling ball and various other things were there.

Lisa organized a garage sale and most of those things were put out for that. We filled the trunk of my car with books, some mine and some Steve's. We took them to a book store that accepted donations of books. Lisa helped me to either get rid of things in the house, or put them in the garage sale. We had lived there for almost twenty years and had accumulated a lot of stuff. What an immense help Lisa and her husband were.

After we had built the new garage, we remodeled the original one car garage into an office for Louie. It also had a large closet in it full of stuff. Lisa helped me go through all that, but Louie's paperwork and records were left for me to go through later. There were a lot of papers that needed to be shredded, and lots to take out to the recycle bin.

I went through the closets, desks, and files. Clothing that I no longer wanted was taken to a thrift shop. I was getting rid of stuff right up until moving day came. Mark came down again to help with packing and to drive me to Wisconsin. Once again he went much more than the extra mile.

The day before the move, I had to have a root canal in the morning, and the crown put on in the afternoon. While I was at the dentist, the packers came and finished the packing. Mark packed all my books and my special china and glassware that had been my grandmother's. I packed my linens and some other personal things.

THE MOVE TO WISCONSIN

Rugie was fourteen and a half years old and I wondered how the move would affect him. I asked the veterinarian about it, and he said Rugie would be alright as long as he was with me. However, that did not prove to be correct. Except for the short time Rugie lived with Steve when he was a puppy, Rugie had lived with us. All he ever knew was our place and that was his territory for over fourteen years. We had over two acres of land which Rugie and I both loved to walk through. Every evening I walked him up and down the road. The smallest lots were at least an acre, and the homes were set back from the road. There were still some wild areas, and Rugie loved the privacy of doing his business behind the bushes. His last activity of the day was to patrol the lot lines on both sides of the house all the way up to the street like a security guard. Then we could all go to bed.

I was not prepared for what I would encounter the day of the move. Mark and I were packing the car and doing last minute things. The new owners were anxious for us to leave, and we were both tired. My back was aching by the time we left, so I stopped at the chiropractor on the way out of town. We got as far as Venice, Florida and stopped for the day. Meanwhile Rugie had not gone potty any of the places we stopped. Mark was worn to a frazzle, and I was exhausted.

We got a hotel room which was on the third floor. Rugie was on a leash that would unwind as he walked ahead. Being so tired, I did not think to set it so that it would not unwind. As we walked off of the elevator, Mark and I were looking for our room and did not notice that Rugie had fallen down a whole flight of stairs that was next to the elevator. Rugie had never seen or been on stairs. Not knowing what they were, he tumbled down the whole staircase, much to my horror. He was lying on the landing and Mark ran down the stairs to get him and brought him back up. I had no idea of the extent he was hurt. Since he was able to walk, we didn't think any bones were broken.

Mark went out to get some food while I rested for a little while. Rugie kept standing by the door. I knew he must have needed to go out, since he hadn't gone potty since we left Naples. There was a subdivision behind the hotel where I took him for a walk, but he wouldn't go. We walked and walked for a long time, and then he started trying to go up the walkway to a house. He did this repeatedly until I realized that he was trying to go home. He evidently thought he had to be home to go potty, as that was all he knew. He must have been very confused. Fourteen and a half years for a dog is about equivalent to ninety years old for a human. When I realized that he wanted to go home so he could go potty, something just snapped in me. I wanted to take him home so badly, but I could not. I felt terrible. My heart ached. I wished I had never sold the house. I became very depressed. Too tired to walk anymore, I took him back to the room. As soon as we were inside, he tinkled. I just threw a towel under him and said, "go for it Rugie." I was relieved that he was relieved. He must have thought that this was his territory.

We struggled with this problem all the way to Wisconsin. We frequently stopped at rest areas along the way where there were special areas for dogs. We thought he might be stimulated to go where other dogs were going, but he wasn't. So Mark would take him to another area, and just walk him until he went.

While I was getting the house ready to sell, my daughter Lisa was looking for a place for me to move into up there that would not be far from her. She went to considerable effort to find a place and make preparations for me. She put a lot of time and energy into it, and even got me enrolled in a senior planning group.

The movers arrived ahead of us, so when we got to the new place, all the furniture had been moved in and arranged. When I went in and sat down, all my emotions spilled out and I started to bawl "I want to go home." I just wanted to go home and that was impossible. After all the work my precious daughter did, my outburst was a disappointment. Oh how I wish I could have kept those emotions under control, but I just lost it. It was really the first time I cried since my husband died. There was so much to deal with that there was no time to grieve. Of course we later discussed the situation, and Lisa was very understanding. I expressed my appreciation for all her hard work. The place she had found was a town house which was very nice. There were three in a row, and mine was in the middle. I especially liked the wild area back behind the townhouses.

Shortly after moving in, the neighbor on one side of me came to my door. There stood an elderly gentleman. He offered to help me if I needed any help. I couldn't think of anything at the moment, but I said I would let him know if I did. Not long after that I was walking my dog after church when he came home from church, and he asked me to have lunch with him. I said yes and he took me to a very nice place for lunch. He was a widower and quite a bit older than I, but he seemed very kind, and very much a gentleman.

Then one day I thought of something he might help me with. I had an appointment in Milwaukee, and did not like driving in the city, so I asked him if he would be able to drive me. He said he liked to drive, and would be most happy to take me. After that, he drove me to my appointments in the city, and we both enjoyed the company. We lived in a small town in a rural area and did not have to drive far to be out in the beautiful Wisconsin countryside. He belonged to the YMCA in a nearby city and invited me to go as his guest one day, which I did. It was wonderful to go swimming which was something I missed very much. Back home in Florida, I swam everyday, which was very good for my back.

On another day, he invited me to go to a park on Lake Michigan. It is a beautiful park and I enjoyed going. Yet as I looked out over the lake, I felt so homesick for Florida.

My neighbor, Jim, and I were becoming good friends. Still, there was a feeling of depression.

The first Sunday after I arrived in Wisconsin, I began to attend the non-denominational church located very close to where I lived. That day a very precious sister in the Lord befriended me. She was one of the leaders of the women's ministry, and very kind and compassionate. She offered to show me around the town. I got in her car, and off we went. After a tour of the town, she took me to her house and made me feel so welcome. She invited me to come to the ladies' Bible study, which I did, and attended until I moved back to Florida. There I met some very wonderful Christian sisters.

Still, that feeling of depression continued.

Not long after we arrived in Wisconsin, Rugie became quite ill. It seemed that he picked up some kind of intestinal flu at one of the doggie rest areas where we stopped. I took him to the veterinarian, but I cannot remember what treatment was prescribed. He did not eat for days, and I was very concerned about him. During this time, my neighbor on the other side invited me for lunch. At first I said yes, but then I told her that my dog was very sick, and I didn't want to leave him alone. She said that I should bring him over too, so I did. She was just the most friendly, wonderful neighbor anyone could ever have, and a fantastic cook to boot. I was enjoying the lunch, and happy to be getting to know my other neighbor. Then suddenly, I noticed Ruger. He was sitting very quietly near us, not trying to get my attention, not begging. He had not eaten for days, and I sensed he would like to eat. I can't believe I did what I did. I asked my sweet neighbor, Ann, if I could give Rugie some table scraps and she said yes. I did and Rugie ate them. I was so glad to see him eat that I almost cried. I had explained the situation to her, and she was so sympathetic. In fact, she offered to give him the leftover food. She had made steak and mashed potatoes which Rugie just loved. I knew he wouldn't care for the salad and vegetables, but he ate the steak and mashed potatoes. After that, Rugie recovered, and I always told Ann it was because of her steak and mashed potatoes. I told her she was our angel. She didn't like dogs, but she liked Rugie. She even took care of him one day when I had to be away. So I was getting to know both of my neighbors, Ann and Jim. Still, that feeling of depression continued.

Louie passed away the end of February. Less than six months later, I had sold the house and moved to Wisconsin. I missed Louie, our home in Naples, and my life there, even though I was glad to be near my daughter. The barn where she boarded her horse was very close to my townhouse, so I went there when she was having her dressage lessons. I enjoyed watching her ride and being near her. Recently, she and I were talking about how one could have that feeling of depression, or whatever it is, and still be happy about the good things in life. Maybe it is a lot of big changes, coupled with loss, that is so difficult.

Earlier I spoke of the physical therapist I was going to in Florida who has skills I never even heard of before I went to her. One of them is integrated manual therapy. This includes myofascial release, myofascial mapping, muscle energy technique, advanced training in craniosacral therapy, advanced training in visceral manipulation, advanced lymphatic drainage, and biologic analogs for the brain, heart and pelvis. In the past five years, she has had over seven hundred hours of continuing education in these therapies. Even if I could explain what each of these therapies are, it is not the intent of this writing. My purpose is to illustrate the fact that she has qualifications that the average physical therapist does not have, but which have been extremely beneficial to me.

Before moving to Wisconsin, I contacted a physical therapist there who was not too far from where I would be living. I asked if she could do integrated manual therapy, and she said that she could do it. After I moved and started going to her, I discovered that she could not. In fact, she actually caused a back sprain by doing the wrong thing.

The area where I lived was a small town in a rural area in southern Wisconsin. I tried every physical therapist within a reasonable distance from my place that I could go to and return home the same day, but had no success. That is when I started thinking about going back to Naples.

ANOTHER LOSS

In the meantime, I received a telephone call from my brother Glen's wife letting me know that my younger brother, Dennis, had lung cancer and did not have long to live. I was shocked! I had no idea. Evidently, his wife felt that I already had enough to cope with and did not wish to add to it. By the time I contacted my brother, he was so very ill that he did not wish to see anyone, and died a short time later. I felt so very sad. My brother Glen and his wife Pat came down from Eagle River in northern Wisconsin for the funeral. I had not seen them since Mom's funeral. I'm glad we could say goodbye to our brother together.

Still, that feeling of depression continued.

WHAT TO DO

I continued to think and pray about moving back to Florida. Meanwhile, I had some great visits with my cousins and one cousin's daughter. They are all strong Christians, and it was a joy to see them.

Then came December; we had a blizzard with eleven inches of snow. In the morning, I opened the door to take Rugie out. He had never seen snow before and looked very startled. He took one step into the snow and would not go any farther. He was totally confused and wanted to go back in the house. He didn't want any part of that snow. We went back into the house and I called Lisa. She and Seamus came over. He shoveled snow off of the grass while Lisa coaxed Ruger with some chicken I had cooked, while they were on the way over. Being tremendously patient with animals, she continued working with him for quite some time until she finally got results.

After the snow storm, the weather turned very cold. As I walked Rugie for our evening outing before going to bed, I was cold to the bone. It was three degrees above zero. Although I was wearing several layers of clothes and my daughter's down coat, I was freezing. Rugie was perplexed, as there was not one blade of grass to be found.

I was praying. My sisters in the Lord at church were praying for guidance for me regarding whether or not I should move back to Florida.

One day Lisa came over with her notebook, and we made two lists. One was for reasons to stay, and one was for reasons to leave. The main reason to stay was to be near Lisa, yet the other list was longer. As it turned out, I did return to Florida.

Mark again helped me with moving, and drove me back to Naples. Less than three months after I moved back, my neighbor, Jim, from Wisconsin moved back to Florida as well. He needed to get out of the cold, so he vacationed in Naples in January and February. During that time, he went back to Cape Coral where he had lived for over twenty years, and found a house to rent just down the street from where he had lived before. I had no idea he was planning to move back to Florida too. It was so nice to see him again.

RUGIE'S PASSING

Four months after I moved back to Naples, my wonderful dog, Rugie, died.

Shortly after we arrived in Naples, Rugie had trouble with his hind legs going out from under him, and he would fall down. Sometimes he was not able to get back up. I took him to the veterinarian who gave him a pain injection. He said it was just to give me more time. Then one day I was about to leave to go for my physical therapy when he fell trying to get to the door. I frantically called Lois Grider, crying that I felt it was time to put Rugie down. She and her husband agreed to come over and go with me to the vet for moral support. When they arrived, Rugie seemed much better. He was walking just fine, so we all decided not to proceed with our plans.

However two nights later, Rugie began to go downhill rapidly. Late that night, he went to the door to go out, and collapsed right over the threshold. I managed to push him back in, but I did not know how I could let him out. I did not want him to collapse outside, because I could not pick him back up and get him inside. It was too late at night to call someone. I had only been living in this place for four months and didn't really know anyone. I had met one person in my new neighborhood. I went to their door but there was no answer. It was quite late. I was up with my precious dog all night as he would try to go out, but I would go as far as the door and bring him back to the living room. He would just fall to the floor. He was dying. I could not wait until morning to get help. I prayed all night that the Lord would take him. Finally morning came. I ran down the street to see if anyone was about. I saw a man in his garage. I told him that my dog was dying, and asked him if he would come over and put Rugie in my car. He did, and I hurried off to the veterinarian. When I arrived and told the veterinarian that Rugie was in the back seat of my car dying, he came out and gave him a sedative or relaxant or something. I had a waterproof cover over the seat and a blanket on top. Rugie finally was relieved after holding his water all night. The veterinarian said he would come back in a few minutes and administer whatever they give to euthanize him. During that time, I knelt down on the pavement to say goodbye to him. He looked at me with such sad eyes. I told him he was going to go to his Creator and that Steve would take care of him until the Lord Jesus Christ brings me home too. Then the veterinarian came back, and in a few minutes, my wonderful companion was gone. Agonizing pain shot through me. I felt so alone. For almost fifteen years, he had brought me so much joy.

My husband had been what they call a workaholic, so companionship with him was scarce. He had to be busy all the time. I was so glad to have Rugie. He was my faithful companion.

In just a little over a year, I lost my husband, left my home of almost twenty years, lost my brother and my dog.

That feeling of depression continued.

I felt so uprooted, so disconnected, so alone. For the first time in my life, I was living alone. I didn't know where I belonged.

A NEW BEGINNING

Through all these ups and downs, I continued giving the first fruits of my day to the Lord. Even though I had difficulty concentrating after my husband's death, my daily scripture reading and prayer time remained constant from the time I received Jesus Christ as my Lord and Savior. He is my Lifeline, the Anchor of my soul. He changes not and He will never leave me or forsake me. He is my Strong Tower, my Defender, a Shield around me, my Glory and the Lifter of my head. The times when I was in the depths of sorrow and despair, He was there. The times when I was in pain, He was there. During the good times, He was there. He is the Good Shepherd. He is the Way, the Truth and the Life and I held on to Him. There is no other way. Although I felt alone, I knew I was not alone. Although it seemed as though there was no way, He was making a way. He is Faithful and True.

My move back to Naples was in December of 2006. Earlier I related that my next door neighbor in Wisconsin, Jim, vacationed in Naples in January and February. While there he visited his old neighborhood in Cape Coral, where he had lived for twenty one years. Cape Coral is about forty miles north of Naples. Just two blocks down the street from the house he once owned, he found a furnished home for rent and rented it. He moved into it in March. One day he drove down from Cape Coral, picked me up and drove back there to show me the house he had rented. It was a large house with a pool. Really nice. He invited me to visit him there anytime.

Meantime my dear friend and sister in the Lord, Lois Grider, saw an ad in the paper for a job that she thought I might be interested in. I applied for it; I was hired and started working as a care-giver.

Jim invited me to come up to Cape Coral and visit him on the weekends. The house he rented was large and very lovely. I had half a house to myself, my own bedroom, my own bathroom. Jim was and is a perfect gentleman. He always took me to a nice place for dinner, and he always found interesting things for us to do. Every weekend we took a walk at the Four Mile Cove or at the Six Mile Cypress Slough.

The Four Mile Cove is an ecological preserve. "It is the only significant wetland left in eastern Cape Coral. The preserve contains 365 acres of white, red and black mangroves along with large open areas of marshlands. There are 5000 feet of shoreline on the Caloosahatchee River and several small tidal streams meandering into the interior" (Ecological Preserve Trail Guide) It is a beautiful and fascinating place. From the boardwalk, one can view the beauty of the preserve.

The Six Mile Cypress Slough in Fort Myers is also a preserve. It is over 3,400 acres of wetland that is about 11 miles long and 1/3 mile wide. It is a wildlife habitat for numerous plant and animal species.

Another thing we enjoyed doing was to go to the Calusa Nature Center and Planetarium. At the center there is the Living Natural History Museum, a Butterfly Aviary, an Audubon Aviary, an insectarium, a picnic area and a gift shop. There are nature trails too.

Jim always found something interesting and enjoyable to do.

When I first started going up there on weekends, I was still feeling very sad and still taking the antidepressant that my doctor prescribed after my husband died. But I tried to never let it show when I was with Jim.

I looked forward to the weekend and going to Jim's place. After a while, I began to forget taking the antidepressant. I was enjoying Jim's companionship and all the different activities so much. I felt that I had come alive again. I told my physical therapist that I was so happy that I kept forgetting to take the medication. I was happy, very happy being with Jim. I always thought of him as a friend, a very good friend. And so it was for three years. One day I was thanking the Lord for Jim's friendship and saying that he was such a dear friend, but that I could never have feelings beyond that. Well, never say never to the Lord! As it turned out, I began to care for Jim in a greater way. The depression was gone! I was very happy, and I did not mind about him being quite a bit older than I. I confided this to a few very close friends. One day my sister in the Lord and very dear friend, Roberta Kiszer, and I were in the car on the way to go out for dinner. We were talking about my relationship with Jim when suddenly the Lord instructed Roberta to pray a specific thing. As she went into very powerful prayer, I began to receive intercession. The Lord was giving me travail and birthing. (See my book Travail, Powerful, Super-

<u>natural Prayer</u>) It was not the first time I received intercession while driving, and I am convinced that, at such times, I receive divine help and protection from the Lord. Roberta and I prayed until the Spirit lifted, and we knew we were finished.

I met Roberta when my late husband and I first moved to Florida. She invited me to the Aglow meeting and I was so glad to be back in Aglow again. Roberta is a very talented and accomplished pianist. For many years she faithfully played piano for praise and worship at the Aglow meetings. She still does, as well as teaching piano in the studio in her home. She also teaches English to immigrants at a local high school. Over the years, Roberta and I prayed together many times and were very close friends.

Around that time, another very dear sister in the Lord called me on the phone about something the Lord had put on her heart to pray, for regarding Jim and I. So we prayed accordingly.

I began asking the Lord if Jim and I should get married. I was happy being with him, and his age just didn't matter. He was always such a gentleman, very considerate and very easy going. I felt a wonderful peace.

My prayers continued as I sought the Lord's will regarding Jim and me. He answered my question about Jim and me getting married with two confirmations. The first one was very personal. The second one was really neat. He showed me a vision that I had in one of our Waterways prayer meetings. (See my book <u>Travail, Powerful, Supernatural Prayer</u>)

Waterways was a prayer meeting that started with sister Patty Cushman and myself. We met once a week. Each time we put on worship music as we waited quietly upon the Lord. Soon we were in His presence.

The following is a quote from my book on travail. "I was already receiving intercession when Patty put the worship music on. The Spirit drew me deeper into powerful travail. I felt that I had been transported to a heavenly realm. My whole being was bathed in His holy presence for I don't know how long.

I saw a golden censer. Then I saw the Lord and the pots filled with water and watched as the Lord was turning the water into wine. It was like watching a video. There was such a presence of the Lord and His power."

Changing the water into wine was the first miracle Jesus did at the wedding of Cana in Galilee. The story is found in John 2:3, 5-10.

3 And when they ran out of wine, the mother of Jesus said to Him, 'They have no wine.'

5 His mother said to the servants, 'Whatever He says to you, do it.'

6 Now there were set there six waterpots of stone, according to the manner of purification of the Jews, containing twenty or thirty gallons apiece.

7 Jesus said to them,'Fill the waterpots with water' and they filled them up to the brim.

8 And He said to them, 'Draw some out now, and take it to the master of the feast.' And they took it.

9 When the master of the feast had tasted the water that was made wine, and did not know where it came from (but the servants who had drawn the water knew), the master of the feast called the bridegroom.

10 And he said to him, 'Every man at the beginning sets out the good wine, and when the guests have well drunk, then the inferior.

You have kept the good wine until now!'
(NKJV)

When the vision ended, I heard the Lord say "I have saved the best until last." Wow!!!! There was no doubt about it. I knew that I knew, that the Lord had put Jim and me together.

We said our vows on August 28, 2010. I have been so happy being with Jim, and I thank God for every day we have together.

When I think about it in retrospect, the Lord had everything prepared for me: the place my daughter found for me to live, and Jim already living right next door. The Lord was making the way for me although I was not aware of it. He is our Way Maker.

Yes, we do go through emotional pain and physical pain too. Yes, there are things in life that hurt. Jesus promises to never leave us or forsake us. (Hebrews 13:5b) And when we can't anymore, He carries us.

It always bothers me when I hear someone blaming God when something bad happens. Jesus made it very clear that we have an enemy who steals, kills and destroys. Let us hold on to God,

Who is for us. "Blessed be the God and Father of our Lord Jesus Christ, the Father of mercies and God of all comfort, who comforts us in all our tribulation," 2 Corinthians 1:3,4a (NKJV)

I thank God for saving my life not once, but four times, for being with me through the good times and the not so good times, for His faithfulness, for His goodness and mercy, for His grace, and most of all for the great gift of salvation and eternal life with Him!

1 Bless the Lord, O my soul; And all that is within me, bless His holy name!

2 Bless the Lord, O my soul, And forget not all His benefits:

3 Who forgives all your iniquities, Who heals all your diseases,

4 Who redeems your life from destruction, Who crowns you with lovingkindness and tender mercies,

5 Who satisfies your mouth with good things, So that your youth is renewed like the eagle's."

Psalm 103:1-5 (NKJV)

114